THE FA OFFICIAL
ENGLAND WOMEN'S
FACT FILE

THE ULTIMATE GUIDE TO THE MIGHTY LIONESSES!

WELBECK

CONTENTS

INTRODUCTION

The FA Official England Women's Fact File celebrates the achievements of the amazing players who have represented the nation since the team's first official match kicked off in 1972.

In this book, you will read about legendary Lionesses from past seasons, meet today's talented squad and discover young players tipped to be future stars. One thing they all share is the feeling of pride each time they have pulled on the shirt bearing the Three Lions.

Included are all the important facts, stats and records, so whether you are a lifelong England fan or are just joining the squad members on their journey, a feast of football awaits. Look back at England's performances at the FIFA Women's World Cup and the UEFA Women's EUROs and discover more memorable moments in the Lionesses' history.

Fifty years on from their official debut, and with a home EUROs to contest in 2022, the future of the current England side has never looked brighter.

BUILDING THE DREAM

Women's football in England was huge during and after the First World War, drawing crowds of more than 50,000 fans in a golden age for the sport. But from 1921 to 1971 women were banned from playing on pitches that belonged to member clubs of the FA, as the game was deemed "quite unsuitable for females".

Momentum for women to play again began to build after the England Men's victory at the 1966 FIFA World Cup, but it wasn't until 1972 that England Women kicked off their first official match. Pitches and facilities were poor, kits and equipment were second hand and women were not paid to play for their country – until as recently as 2009. It was clear that many strides were needed to be taken to make up for those lost 50 years.

Although the ban in the women's game rippled across Europe, the wilderness years had put England's rivals a few steps ahead. England Women qualified for just one of the first four FIFA World Cups, while they have yet to win a UEFA Women's European Championship.

Over the short history of the England Women football team, a host of pioneers – players, coaches, officials and more incredible women and men behind the scenes – have helped pave the way for the next generation of women and girls to play the game they love. Now women in football can play professionally, and England can boast one of the strongest women's international teams in the world. The Lionesses play with passion, pride and for you – the fans.

ENGLAND WOMEN: A TIMELINE

1920 The first unofficial women's international game is played. Dick, Kerr Ladies FC beat a French side 2-0.

1921 The FA bans women from playing on its members' grounds, claiming football is "unsuitable" for females.

1971 Fifty years later, the ban is finally lifted in England.

1972 England Women beat Scotland Women in the team's first official fixture.

1984 England finish as runners-up in a European Competition for women's football, contested by four nations.

1998 Hope Powell is appointed as England Women's first full-time coach.

2005 The 2005 UEFA Women's Championship is played in England, attracting record attendances and millions of TV viewers.

2009 Hope Powell masterminds contracts for England players, paying them a salary for the first time. The team finish as runners-up at the Women's EURO in Finland.

2015 The Lionesses record their best ever run at a World Cup, finishing third in Canada.

2017 England reach another semi-final, at the EURO tournament, hosted by the Netherlands.

2019 England win the SheBelieves trophy and finish fourth at the World Cup in France.

2021 The Lionesses go unbeaten in all of their competitive fixtures, scoring an impressive 53 goals.

2022 England host the UEFA Women's EURO 2022, with support for the team at record levels.

STATS

BORN: 23 April, 1988 (Durham)

POSITION: Defender

CAPS: 121

GOALS: 13

DEBUT APPEARANCE: March 2007 v Russia

DEBUT GOAL: March 2009 v South Africa

STEPH HOUGHTON

Steph's Story

From the moment she could walk, Steph Houghton was always kicking a ball around with her dad, brother or friends in the north-east of England. She was first scouted aged nine, while on a football camp at Sunderland FC during the school holidays. At that time there was no proper academy, so Steph joined the under-16s team.

Steph was barely a teenager in her first season with Sunderland's first team, and then played as a midfielder. Training was part-time, kits were handed down from the men's teams and women had to pay to play. Steph pushed herself hard and in 2007 she won the FA Young Player of the Year award.

Her first senior England call-up came at the age of 17. Under manager Hope Powell, Steph was determined to become a better player – the fittest and best version of herself. But days before the England squad were about to fly out to the World Cup in China, she suffered a devastating leg break in training. Steph worked her way back to fitness, but was seriously injured again just before the Women's EURO 2009 squad was announced. It took two and a half years for her to return to full fitness.

Steph's first taste of a World Cup was in 2011, when she came on as a sub in England's final game of the tournament. EURO 2013 came two years later, but England disappointingly finished bottom of their group. In January 2014, after winning a host of trophies with Arsenal, Steph was named captain of England Women at the age of 25. Steph, now playing in defence, quickly grew into the role, showing strong skills as the Lionesses' leader. It was under her captaincy that England reached their first ever World Cup semi-finals, at the 2015 tournament in

Steph studied Three Lions captain David Beckham growing up, to become superb at set pieces herself.

Canada. In doing so, the team inspired thousands of women, girls and fans to get involved in football.

Steph led England to a second semi-final in a row at Euro 2017, losing out to hosts the Netherlands. Then, in 2018, she earned her 100th international cap. 2019 was an unforgettable year for Steph, now Phil Neville's choice of skipper, and England Women. The defender scored a fantastic free-kick against world champions the USA, earning a point that helped the Lionesses to win the SheBelieves Cup. The World Cup followed that summer, with England again reaching the semi-finals. Steph's goal against Cameroon saw the Lionesses progress to the quarter-finals, but a stronger opponent, the USA, stood firm in the semis. England's dreams of reaching their first World Cup final were ended as Steph saw her penalty saved late in the game. It was heartbreak for England, as the holders went on to win the World Cup.

Steph has always been passionate about inspiring the next generation of young girls and boys to get into football and live their dreams. While she knows her playing career won't last forever, her legacy as a leader of the Lionesses certainly will.

Steph's passion, courage and ability to inspire others shine through, on and off the pitch.

TAKING ON THE WORLD

The biggest competition in women's football is the FIFA Women's World Cup. Held every four years, this famous global tournament sees the best international teams go head to head. England have participated in five editions of the competition, twice reaching the semi-finals. Here's how they've fared.

SWEDEN 1995

RECORD

 4 MATCHES PLAYED

 6 GOALS SCORED

 LEADING SCORERS:
GILLIAN COULTHARD & KAREN FARLEY (2)

CARDS:

▢ 4

■ 0

The second official World Cup was held in Sweden, a pioneering nation of women's football. Twelve teams played in the tournament, as England made their debut alongside Australia and Canada. An opening win against Canada was followed by defeat to the eventual champions, Norway. England's final group match was a 3-2 win over Nigeria, as they battled their way through to the knockout stages as group runners-up. Next up were Germany in the quarter-finals, a match that gave birth to a rivalry between the nations that was all too familiar in the men's game. The Lionesses lost 3-0, as Germany progressed to the semis.

CHINA 2007

Following a 12-year absence, England qualified for their second World Cup in China. Captained by Faye White, the Lionesses' star-studded squad included Kelly Smith, Fara Williams and Jill Scott. An opening 2-2 draw with Japan was followed by a goalless game against Germany, before a 6-1 win over Argentina sealed England's place in the final eight. There they faced two-time winners the USA, whose three second-half goals ended the Lionesses' run in the competition.

The Lionesses celebrate one of six goals scored against Argentina.

RECORD

- **4** MATCHES PLAYED
- **8** GOALS SCORED
- **LEADING SCORERS:**
  KELLY SMITH (4)
- **CARDS:**
  - ☐ 4
  - ■ 0

GERMANY 2011

Four years later, the tournament was hosted by the reigning champions, Germany. This time, England topped their group, beating New Zealand and Japan, after a nervy opening draw with Mexico. Fara Williams and Ellen White were among the goalscorers. France were England's next opponents in the quarter-finals. A Jill Scott goal put the Lionesses ahead, but Les Bleues equalised with just two minutes to go. Extra time was played, but as neither team could break the deadlock, the match went to penalties, where England sadly lost by a single spot-kick.

RECORD

- **4** MATCHES PLAYED
- **6** GOALS SCORED
- **LEADING SCORER:**
  JILL SCOTT (2)

CARDS:
- ☐ 5
- ■ 0

CANADA 2015

The seventh edition of the FIFA Women's World Cup saw 24 nations enter the competition for the first time. England kicked off against France – the team that had eliminated the Lionesses four years earlier – and again it was a Eugénie Le Sommer goal that handed France the victory. Wins against Mexico and Colombia followed though, to see England safely through to the knockout rounds.

RECORD

7 MATCHES PLAYED

10 GOALS SCORED

LEADING SCORER:
FARA WILLIAMS (3)

CARDS:
8
0

GROUP MATCHES:

FRANCE	1-0	**ENGLAND**
ENGLAND	2-1	MEXICO

KIRBY (70), CARNEY (81)

ENGLAND	2-1	COLOMBIA

CARNEY (14), WILLIAMS (37, PEN)

Skipper Steph Houghton led England at a major tournament for the first time.

The Knockout Stages

A stunning Lucy Bronze strike knocked out Norway in the round of 16, before two early goals secured an impressive quarter-final victory over hosts Canada. It was the first time the Lionesses had reached a World Cup semi-final in their history.

ROUND OF 16:

NORWAY   1-2   **ENGLAND**
HOUGHTON (60), BRONZE (75)

QUARTER-FINALS:

ENGLAND   2-1   CANADA
TAYLOR (10), BRONZE (13)

Next, England faced reigning champions Japan. With a penalty apiece scored, the match looked to be heading for extra time. What followed in injury time proved to be heartbreak for the Lionesses, as an unlucky Laura Bassett own goal saw Japan run out the winners.

SEMI-FINALS:

JAPAN   2-1   **ENGLAND**   WILLIAMS (39, PEN)

The Lionesses' pride was restored in the play-off for third place, as England put in a spirited performance. It took an extra-time Fara Williams penalty for Mark Sampson's side to beat Germany for the first time. To the delight of the fans who watched the match back home, England returned from Canada wearing bronze medals.

Fara Williams celebrates England's triumph against Germany in the third place play-off match at the 2015 FIFA Women's World Cup.

THIRD PLACE PLAY-OFF:

GERMANY   0-1   **ENGLAND**   WILLIAMS (107, PEN)

FRANCE 2019

In 2019, France hosted the biggest World Cup yet, with thrilling matches, packed stadiums and more than a billion television viewers worldwide. With their forwards firing, England took maximum points in their group matches. Classy performances against Scotland, Argentina and rivals Japan put the Lionesses at the top of Group D.

RECORD

- **7** MATCHES PLAYED
- **13** GOALS SCORED
- **LEADING SCORER:** ELLEN WHITE (6)

CARDS:
- ☐ 2
- ■ 1

Ellen White just couldn't stop scoring in the race for the Golden Boot.

GROUP MATCHES:

ENGLAND	2-1	SCOTLAND
👟 PARRIS (14, PEN), WHITE (40)

ENGLAND	1-0	ARGENTINA
👟 TAYLOR (62)

JAPAN	2-0	**ENGLAND**
👟 WHITE (14, 84)

The Knockout Stages

The round of 16 tie against Cameroon was a fiery affair! Goals from captain Steph Houghton, Ellen White and Alex Greenwood confirmed Cameroon's exit, as England progressed to the quarter-finals. The Lionesses proved too good for their next opponents, Norway, as another Lucy Bronze thunderbolt capped a fine performance. England had reached the final four in back-to-back World Cups.

ROUND OF 16:

ENGLAND 3-0 CAMEROON
👟 HOUGHTON (14), WHITE (45+4), GREENWOOD (58)

QUARTER-FINALS:

NORWAY 0-3 **ENGLAND**
👟 SCOTT (3), WHITE (40), BRONZE (57)

Lucy Bronze is mobbed by her teammates after scoring again against Norway – a strike that won goal of the tournament.

England's dream of reaching a first World Cup final was shattered in their semi-final against holders, the USA. Christen Press and Alex Morgan headers either side of an Ellen White strike put the USA 2-1 ahead at half-time. Despite a strong England response in the second-half, luck was ultimately against the Lionesses: VAR ruled a second goal from White offside literally by a toe's length, while a late Steph Houghton penalty was saved.

SEMI-FINALS:

ENGLAND 1-2 UNITED STATES 👟 WHITE (19)

With bronze medals up for grabs against Sweden, Phil Neville's side headed to Nice. With keeper Karen Bardsley out injured and defender Millie Bright suspended, England finally ran out of steam. A curled finish from Kirby gave England hope, but another Ellen White goal was cancelled out by VAR and England Women had to settle for fourth place.

THIRD PLACE PLAY-OFF:

ENGLAND 1-2 SWEDEN
👟 KIRBY (31)

17

LUCY BRONZE

STATS

BORN: 28 October, 1991
(Berwick-upon-Tweed)

POSITION: Defender

CAPS: 83

GOALS: 9

DEBUT APPEARANCE:
June 2013 v Japan

DEBUT GOAL: June 2014 v
Belarus

Lucy's Story

Born Lucia Roberta Tough Bronze to an English mother and Portuguese father, Lucy grew up on Holy Island and then Alnwick in the north-east of England. Her first ambition growing up was to be better at football than her older brother, Jorge.

Lucy joined Jorge's boys' team, Alnwick Town, ignoring those who told her that being strong and competitive was not 'girly'. She was determined to be the best. At the age of 11, she suffered her first setback in the sport, when she was forced to quit the team as FA regulations at the time did not allow girls and boys to play together beyond this age. Lucy wasn't to be deterred and travelled more than an hour each way to train with Sunderland's Academy. It was here that Lucy, who admits that she struggled with shyness growing up, played alongside future England Women stars Lucy Staniforth, Demi Stokes and Jordan Nobbs, and found friendships through football.

Her next team would be based much further from home, as Lucy earned a university scholarship to play for the Tar Heels in North Carolina, USA. She returned to Sunderland briefly before a move to WSL side Everton in 2010. Lucy juggled her studies at university and a job in a takeaway pizza shop, with playing in the newly formed WSL and the UEFA Champions League! By this time, she was also representing England at Under-19 level.

Disaster then struck, as the defender had to fight back from two serious knee injuries. The most challenging period in her career, Lucy was even told that she might never play for England again. But "Tough" by middle name, tough by nature, Lucy trained by herself to regain full fitness. She was finally given her senior debut for England in 2013, and made the squad for the EUROs in Sweden that same year.

Lucy celebrates with team-mate Jordan Nobbs after opening her goal-scoring account with a stunning strike at the 2015 World Cup.

Lucy announced herself on the global stage during the World Cup in Canada 2015, with a stunning hit in the round-of-16 victory over Norway, as well as the winner against hosts Canada in the quarter-finals. She was rewarded for her performances with a place in the tournament's "All-Star Squad".

Since then her progress has been nothing short of remarkable, as Lucy has established herself among the world's very best players, winning the Silver Ball at the 2019 World Cup and a UEFA Women's Player of the Year Award. In 2020, Lucy was announced as FIFA's Best Women's Player of the Year, yet the defender modestly says that her hard work outweighs her talent. Her fans meanwhile know that Lucy is, without doubt, one of the finest players in England Women's history.

A leader on the pitch, Lucy first captained the England senior side at the 2018 SheBelieves Cup.

EURO HEROES

The top women's European nations compete every four years at the UEFA Women's Championship. England alongside three other nations competed in the original tournament in 1984. Sixteen teams now feature in the competition.

EURO 1984

RECORD

- ⚽ **4** MATCHES PLAYED
- ⚽ **4** GOALS SCORED
- 👟 **LEADING SCORER:** LINDA CURL (2)
- 🏆 **POSITION:** FINAL

The '1984 European Competition for Women's Football' was held in six host cities across Europe, with matches lasting 70 minutes. England, Denmark, Sweden and Italy took part, with England and Sweden reaching the two-legged final unbeaten. Sweden won their home leg 1-0 and England did the same in the reverse fixture, before a penalty shoot-out saw Sweden crowned champions.

EURO 1987

The same four nations qualified for the next tournament, held in Norway. Again, England lost to Sweden, who scored an extra-time goal to win the match 3-2. Italy then beat England 2-1 in the play-off for third place.

RECORD

- ⚽ **2** MATCHES PLAYED
- ⚽ **3** GOALS SCORED
- 👟 **LEADING SCORER:** KERRY DAVIS (2)
- 🏆 **POSITION:** SEMI-FINALS

The captains shake hands before the 1984 final kicks off between England and Sweden.

EURO 1995

It was not until 1995 that England qualified for their next European Championship, held across Europe. This time, England, Germany, Norway and Sweden made up the four teams, as England took on Germany over two legs. Germany won both matches, 1-4 and 2-1, and went on to bag a hat-trick of titles.

RECORD

🎮 **2** MATCHES PLAYED

⚽ **2** GOALS SCORED

🏆 **POSITION:** SEMI-FINALS

👟 **LEADING SCORER:**
KAREN FARLEY (2)

A young Kelly Smith earns her first England cap in a qualifier for EURO 1995.

EURO 2001

RECORD

🎮 **3** MATCHES PLAYED

⚽ **1** GOAL SCORED

👟 **LEADING SCORER:** ANGELA BANKS (1)

🏆 **POSITION:** QUARTER-FINALS

Eight teams played in the 2001 finals. Old foes Sweden and Germany were in England's group, plus Russia. An opening draw with Russia gave England their only point – and goal – in the tournament, as the Lionesses went down 4-0 to Sweden and 3-0 to Germany. England's victors met again in the final, with Germany claiming their fifth championship.

Luck was not on the side of the Lionesses in 2001.

EURO 2005

Eight teams contested the 2005 finals. Hosts England were matched with Nordic nations Sweden, Finland and Denmark in their group, winning their first match against Finland 3-2. Losses against Sweden and Denmark, though, saw England slump bottom of the group. Germany again breezed to victory in the final, while the tournament drew record crowds in stadiums and on TV.

Right-back Alex Scott takes on a Danish defender.

RECORD

- **3** MATCHES PLAYED
- **4** GOALS SCORED
- **POSITION:** GROUP STAGE
- **LEADING SCORERS:** BARR, CARNEY, WILLIAMS (1)

EURO 2009

Twelve teams featured in the competition held in Finland, with three groups arranged into four teams. Sweden, Italy and Russia completed group C with England. A defeat to Italy was followed by a 3-2 win over Russia, before a draw against Sweden earned England third place in the group – and just enough points to reach the next round.

Germany double up to stop Karen Carney in the final.

RECORD

- **6** MATCHES PLAYED
- **12** GOALS SCORED
- **LEADING SCORERS:** ENI ALUKO, KELLY SMITH (3)
- **POSITION:** RUNNERS-UP

The Knockout Stages

A 3-2 victory over Finland in the quarter-final came next, before a Jill Scott goal in extra-time saw the Lionesses beat the Netherlands 2-1 in the semi-final. England had reached the final for the first time since 1984! But experienced finalists Germany were too strong for England, as the Lionesses crashed to a 6-2 defeat.

EURO 2013

RECORD

⚽ **3** MATCHES PLAYED

⚽ **3** GOALS SCORED

👟 **LEADING SCORERS:**
ALUKO, BASSETT, DUGGAN (1)

🏆 **POSITION:** GROUP STAGE

Sweden hosted the next championship, which saw an early England exit after they finished bottom of the group. Losses against France and Spain meant that England's point versus Russia was not enough to save them. The squad had learned a tough lesson and began a period of rebuilding.

Jodie Taylor celebrates her hat-trick against rivals Scotland at Women's Euro 2017.

Toni Duggan's goal in the group match against Russia earned England's only point.

EURO 2017

RECORD

⚽ **5** MATCHES PLAYED

⚽ **11** GOALS SCORED

👟 **LEADING SCORER:**
JODIE TAYLOR (5)

🏆 **POSITION:**
SEMI-FINALS

Staged in the Netherlands, the competition expanded to feature Europe's top 16 nations. A strong showing saw England top their group, the team keen to learn from their mistakes. Three wins against Scotland, Spain and Portugal set up a quarter-final with France.

The Knockout Stages

When England edged out France with a Jodie Taylor strike, it was the first time they had beaten Les Bleues in 43 years. Their semi-final was a disappointing night, though, as hosts the Netherlands outclassed England, winning 3-0. The dazzling Dutch won a thrilling 4-2 final against Denmark, ending Germany's 22-year reign as champions of Europe.

EURO 2022

England were chosen as hosts for the 2022 championship – the 13th Women's EURO. Sixteen nations have been drawn into four groups of four, with the top two in each section progressing to the knockout phase. Delayed by a year due to the COVID-19 pandemic, the excitement levels are building as a summer of top football action awaits!

Winning the Golden Boot on home soil would be a dream come true for any striker. Just ask Ellen White!

England's Group Matches

England Women head up Group A, and will face Austria, Norway and Northern Ireland in the Group Stage. England know Austria and Northern Ireland well, from the 2023 World Cup qualifying rounds, while the Lionesses eliminated Norway at the 2019 World Cup.

Host Stadiums

Matches will be played at 10 different stadiums up and down the country, giving more fans an opportunity to see the Lionesses live in action, close to home.

MANCHESTER CITY ACADEMY STADIUM, MANCHESTER	OLD TRAFFORD, MANCHESTER	ST. MARY'S STADIUM, SOUTHAMPTON	BRENTFORD COMMUNITY STADIUM, LONDON	COMMUNITY STADIUM, BRIGHTON & HOVE
CAPACITY: 7,000	**CAPACITY:** 75,000	**CAPACITY:** 32,000	**CAPACITY:** 17,000	**CAPACITY:** 30,000
MATCHES: GROUP	**MATCHES:** GROUP	**MATCHES:** GROUP	**MATCHES:** GROUP, QUARTER-FINALS	**MATCHES:** GROUP, QUARTER-FINALS

The UEFA Women's EURO logo inspired the shape and form for the competition trophy, which is 60 cm tall and weighs 6.7 kg.

Quarter-Finals

Finishing top of Group A, or as runners-up, would likely set up a quarter-final tie against either Germany, Spain or Denmark, each one a strong opponent, though Finland could yet spring a surprise.

NEW YORK STADIUM, ROTHERHAM	**LEIGH SPORTS VILLAGE, WIGAN & LEIGH**	**STADIUM MK, MILTON KEYNES**	**BRAMALL LANE, SHEFFIELD**	**WEMBLEY STADIUM, LONDON**
CAPACITY: 12, 000	**CAPACITY:** 12,000	**CAPACITY:** 30,000	**CAPACITY:** 30,000	**CAPACITY:** 90,000
MATCHES: GROUP, QUARTER-FINALS	**MATCHES:** GROUP, QUARTER-FINALS	**MATCHES:** GROUP, SEMI-FINALS	**MATCHES:** GROUP, SEMI-FINALS	**MATCH:** FINAL

NIKITA PARRIS

STATS

BORN: 10 March, 1994 (Liverpool)

POSITION: Forward

CAPS: 57

GOALS: 15

DEBUT APPEARANCE: June 2016 v Serbia

DEBUT GOAL: June 2016 v Serbia

Nikita's Story

It was roughly at the age of six that Nikita Parris's love of football began, playing in the garden with her older brothers, then in the streets outside her house in Toxteth, Liverpool. The following year, a neighbour invited Nikita to play for the all-boys' side he trained, Kingsley United.

It wasn't long before Nikita inspired other girls in her community to play, and at the age of 11 she helped to form a local women's team. At that time, professional football didn't exist for women, but from a young age Nikita always strived to reach the top. She was convinced that by the time she grew up she could earn a living from playing the game. Aged 12, Nikita was recruited by former England Women's manager, Mo Marley, to play for Everton's centre of excellence. Nikita's mother didn't drive and had three more young children to raise alone, so the family were thankful that Mo saw Nikita's potential and collected the youngster for training every session until Nikita was 20.

At Everton, Nikita's game was based on pace and courage, never afraid to take on players above her age group. In 2009, she joined England's under-17s, aged 15. In 2010, Nikita made her senior debut for Everton, in the first season of the professional Women's Super League – Nikita's vision had come true! Champions League football followed.

Nikita made her senior international appearance in June 2016, and scored her first goal that same month, against the same opponent, Serbia. Her first goal at a major tournament, the winner against Portugal, came at EURO 2017, where Nikita's fine forward play helped England reach the semi-finals.

Nikita begins her celebrations after scoring the opening goal against Scotland at the 2019 FIFA Women's World Cup.

By the time the 2019 World Cup squad was announced, Nikita had been a Manchester City player for three years – signing in early 2016 – and was then the WSL's all-time top scorer, an amazing achievement at the age of just 24. England Women and Nikita headed to France full of confidence. In their opening match, Nikita stepped up to score a penalty, a goal that helped to secure the Lionesses' first victory. The team went on to finish fourth in the tournament. Under head coach Sarina Wiegman, Nikita has already netted her first goal, and would be honoured to represent England Women at the home EUROs in 2022. Even though she has passed 50 caps, Nikita admits that she still gets butterflies every time she receives an England call-up. Playing for her country is an honour that Nikita never takes for granted.

Despite her success in the game, Nikita remains a humble player and is quick to encourage aspiring young footballers to strive to be "better than [her]". She can count young players from as far away as China and India among her fans, and is proud that she can share her journey with girls from different ethnicities and of different faiths. In Nikita Parris, England have a Lioness who leads by example.

Nikita is a player who gives her all in an England shirt.

MEET THE SQUAD

Led by head coach Sarina Wiegman, England Women's squad is a perfect blend of youth and experience. Many players have represented the nation at multiple World Cups and European Championships, while others are just beginning their journey. What they all share is a passion to perform as a team and play with pride each time they pull on an England shirt.

Sarina is among the best international coaches in the women's game and will lead England at EURO 2022.

MILLIE BRIGHT

Lioness Lowdown:

A tough defender who's strong in the air, Millie Bright is known for her well-timed tackles and clearances. She's played in two major tournaments with England and hopes to make it a hat-trick at EURO 2022. After waiting five years for her first international goal, Millie scored twice against Luxembourg in a FIFA World Cup qualifier in 2021.

STATS

BORN: 21 August, 1993 (Chesterfield)

POSITION: Defender

CAPS: 47

GOALS: 5

DEBUT APPEARANCE: September 2016 v Belgium

DEBUT GOAL: September 2021 v Luxembourg

GETTING TO KNOW MILLIE
When she's not playing football, Millie loves spending time horse riding.

29

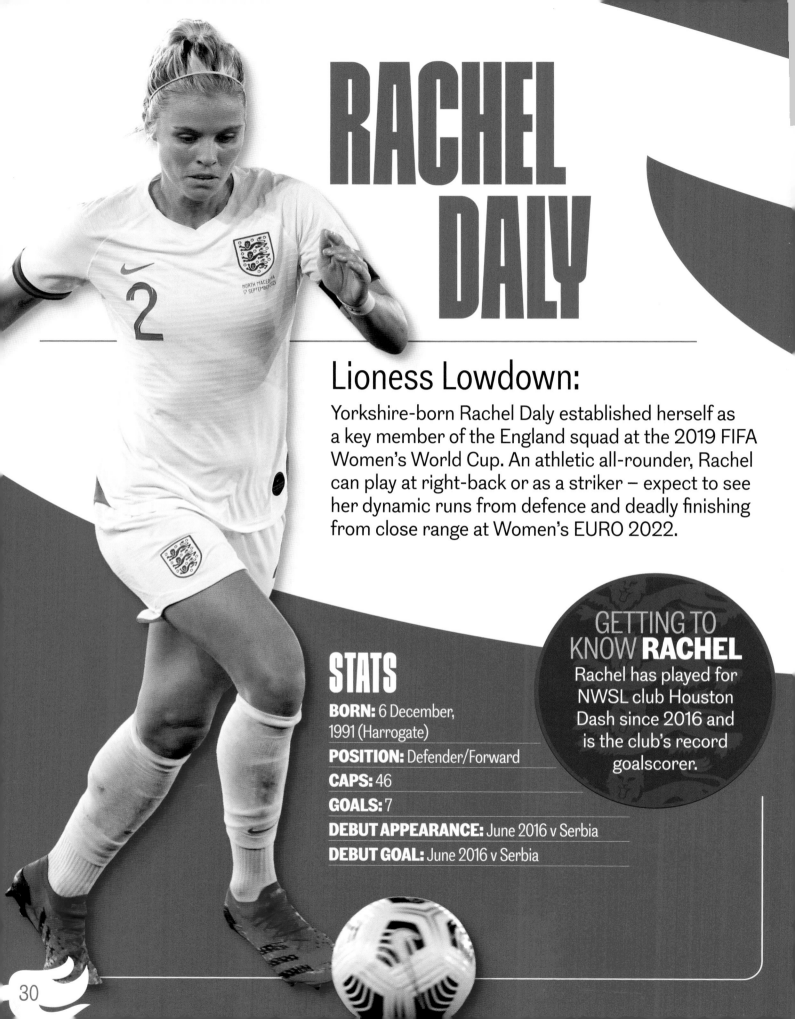

RACHEL DALY

Lioness Lowdown:

Yorkshire-born Rachel Daly established herself as a key member of the England squad at the 2019 FIFA Women's World Cup. An athletic all-rounder, Rachel can play at right-back or as a striker – expect to see her dynamic runs from defence and deadly finishing from close range at Women's EURO 2022.

STATS

BORN: 6 December, 1991 (Harrogate)

POSITION: Defender/Forward

CAPS: 46

GOALS: 7

DEBUT APPEARANCE: June 2016 v Serbia

DEBUT GOAL: June 2016 v Serbia

GETTING TO KNOW **RACHEL**

Rachel has played for NWSL club Houston Dash since 2016 and is the club's record goalscorer.

BETHANY ENGLAND

Lioness Lowdown:

Never has a player had a surname more befitting her national team than Bethany! Forward Beth is always a goal threat, whether she starts the game or comes on as a super sub. A gifted finisher and excellent in the air, Beth has already scored eight goals in her first 15 senior appearances. She has previously played with the U-19 and U-23 England teams.

STATS

BORN: 3 June, 1994 (Barnsley)

POSITION: Forward

CAPS: 15

GOALS: 8

DEBUT APPEARANCE: August 2019 v Belgium

DEBUT GOAL: October 2019 v Brazil

GETTING TO KNOW BETHANY

Beth has twice considered giving up football, but has come back stronger each time.

ALEX GREENWOOD

Lioness Lowdown:

A gifted left-back with fantastic technique, Alex Greenwood is equally comfortable playing as a central defender. She loves to step up for set pieces and is a strong leader on the pitch, too. Alex was the youngest member of the England Women squad at the 2015 Women's World Cup, winning a bronze medal, and has since been selected for Women's EURO 2017 and the 2019 Women's World Cup.

GETTING TO KNOW **ALEX**

Alex's best mate in football is Manchester City and England roommate, Ellie Roebuck.

STATS

BORN: 7 September, 1993 (Liverpool)

POSITION: Defender

CAPS: 45

GOALS: 5

DEBUT APPEARANCE: March 2014 v Italy

DEBUT GOAL: September 2014 v Montenegro

LAUREN HEMP

Lioness Lowdown:

A dynamic young forward with lots of pace, Lauren Hemp is a player with a bright future. She made her England debut in 2019 and is already into double figures for appearances. In 2020, UEFA named Lauren as one of Europe's 10 most promising young players. Watch her take on defenders at her first major tournament with England at Women's EURO 2022.

GETTING TO KNOW **LAUREN**
Lauren played in a boys' team until she was 16 years old.

STATS

BORN: 7 August, 2000 (North Walsham)

POSITION: Forward

CAPS: 17

GOALS: 4

DEBUT APPEARANCE: October 2019 v Portugal

DEBUT GOAL: November 2021 v Latvia

CHLOE KELLY

Lioness Lowdown:

Forward Chloe Kelly first linked up with England's U-15s, rising up through the ranks to earn her first senior cap in 2018. She was part of the squad that won bronze at the FIFA U-20 Women's World Cup in 2018. Chloe is keen to make up for lost time after a serious injury saw her miss a lot of football in 2021.

GETTING TO KNOW **CHLOE**

The youngest of seven siblings, Chloe grew up playing 'cage football' in the west London estate where she lived.

STATS

BORN: 15 January, 1998 (London)

POSITION: Forward

CAPS: 7

GOALS: 0

DEBUT APPEARANCE: November 2018 v Austria

FRAN KIRBY

Lioness Lowdown:

Forward Fran Kirby made a name for herself at the 2015 Women's World Cup in Canada. Playing as a No10, speed, dribbling and cool finishing are in her DNA, while her ball control has fans on their feet. Fran has had to battle injury and illness during her career, but remains one of Europe's finest players when fit. In 2021, Fran won her 50th England cap.

GETTING TO KNOW **FRAN**

In October 2019, Fran received an Honorary Doctorate from the University of Winchester.

STATS

BORN: 29 June, 1993 (Reading)

POSITION: Forward

CAPS: 54

GOALS: 15

DEBUT APPEARANCE: August 2014 v Sweden

DEBUT GOAL: August 2014 v Sweden

BETH MEAD

STATS

BORN: 9 May, 1995 (Whitby)

POSITION: Forward

CAPS: 34

GOALS: 16

DEBUT APPEARANCE: April 2018 v Wales

DEBUT GOAL: September 2018 v Kazakhstan

Lioness Lowdown:

Striker Beth Mead has played for England at every age group, and made her senior debut in 2018. When she's not scoring herself, Beth can play on either wing and enjoys creating chances for others. Her highlights in an England shirt so far include her goals that helped the team win the 2019 SheBelieves Cup. In 2021 she became the first England woman to score a hat-trick at Wembley.

GETTING TO KNOW **BETH**

Beth played all kinds of sports growing up, including cross country and cricket, but football was her first love.

JORDAN NOBBS

Lioness Lowdown:

Fan favourite Jordan Nobbs brings creativity to England's midfield. She can create chances and link the play, and score herself, especially with her long-range shots from outside the box. A serious knee injury saw Jordan miss the 2019 Women's World Cup, while injury limited her to a single match at the 2015 tournament. A start at Women's EURO 2022 would mark a hat-trick of appearances at the European Championships for Jordan, having already starred at Women's EURO 2013 and 2017.

STATS

BORN: 8 December, 1992 (Stockton-on-Tees)

POSITION: Midfielder

CAPS: 67

GOALS: 8

DEBUT APPEARANCE: March 2013 v Italy

DEBUT GOAL: March 2013 v Italy

GETTING TO KNOW JORDAN

Jordan wants to coach after hanging up her boots. She has already begun working towards her coaching qualifications.

37

ELLIE ROEBUCK

Lioness Lowdown:

Ellie Roebuck is terrific at shot-stopping and stays ice-cool playing the ball out from the back. Among the most exciting young keepers in the world, Ellie is competing for the England No1 position against experienced stoppers Carly Telford and Manchester City teammate Karen Bardsley. Women's EURO 2022 presents a great opportunity for Ellie to play at her first major finals in an England shirt.

GETTING TO KNOW **ELLIE**

Ellie is one of a new generation of talented young goalkeepers, with Hannah Hampton and Sandy MacIver waiting in the wings.

STATS

BORN: 23 September, 1999 (Sheffield)

POSITION: Goalkeeper

CAPS: 8

DEBUT APPEARANCE: November 2018 v Austria

JILL SCOTT

STATS

BORN: 2 February, 1987 (Sunderland)

POSITION: Midfielder

CAPS: 153

GOALS: 26

DEBUT APPEARANCE: August 2006 v Netherlands

DEBUT GOAL: October 2006 v Germany

GETTING TO KNOW JILL

Jill loves coffee. So much so that she has opened her own coffee shop in Manchester!

Lioness Lowdown:

Jill Scott is currently the squad's most experienced player, and is second only to Fara Williams among the nation's most capped players of all time. The brilliant box-to-box midfielder has represented England at four Women's World Cups and three European Championships, incredibly scoring at four different tournaments. Quite simply a legend.

LUCY STANIFORTH

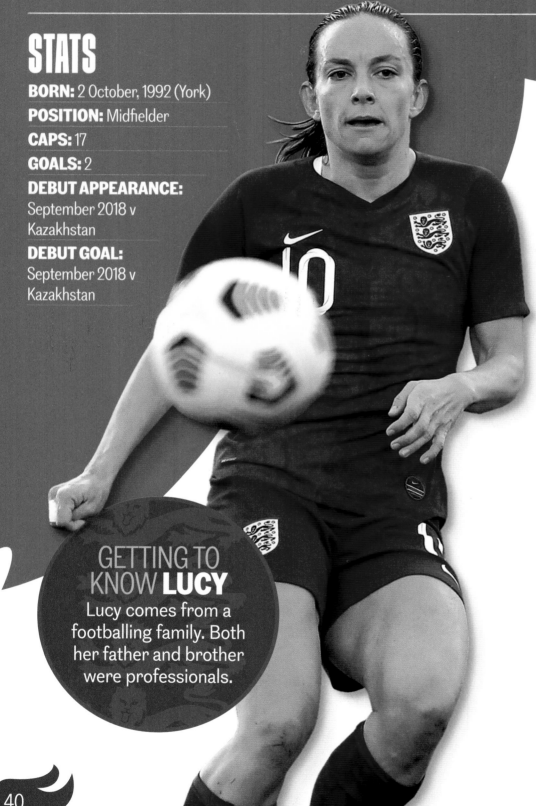

STATS

BORN: 2 October, 1992 (York)
POSITION: Midfielder
CAPS: 17
GOALS: 2
DEBUT APPEARANCE:
September 2018 v
Kazakhstan
DEBUT GOAL:
September 2018 v
Kazakhstan

GETTING TO KNOW **LUCY**
Lucy comes from a footballing family. Both her father and brother were professionals.

Lioness Lowdown:

Attacking midfielder Lucy Staniforth has represented her nation in every age group from England U-17s. Lucy's first highlight in an England shirt was her debut goal, scored just before her 26th birthday. Her most important strike helped the senior side win the 2019 SheBelieves Cup. Lucy promises to give her all to play at Women's EURO 2022 on home soil.

GEORGIA STANWAY

Lioness Lowdown:

Since scoring on her debut as a 19 year-old, young Georgia Stanway has been a regular in the England set-up. Naturally athletic, Georgia is first and foremost a goal-getter, playing as a centre-forward or in midfield, but can also help out in a wing-back role. Still in her early 20s, Georgia's best appearances lie ahead of her.

STATS

BORN: 3 January, 1999 (Barrow-in-Furness)
POSITION: Midfielder/Forward
CAPS: 29
GOALS: 4
DEBUT APPEARANCE: November 2018 v Austria
DEBUT GOAL: November 2018 v Austria

GETTING TO KNOW **GEORGIA**

Georgia never imagined that football would be her career and thought that she'd join the police or the army one day.

DEMI STOKES

STATS

BORN: 12 December, 1991 (Dudley)

POSITION: Defender

CAPS: 64

GOALS: 1

DEBUT APPEARANCE: January 2014 v Norway

DEBUT GOAL: April 2014 v Montenegro

GETTING TO KNOW **DEMI**

Demi's idol growing up was England legend, Rachel Yankey. As a teenager, Demi even got to meet her hero!

Lioness Lowdown:

Demi Stokes' first England call-up came when she was still studying at the University of South Florida. Now, the left-back is one of the most experienced players in the squad. A player with great physical strength and a solid tackler, Demi has played at major finals including Women's EURO 2017 and the 2019 Women's World Cup.

ELLA TOONE

Lioness Lowdown:

Ella Toone was thrilled to have made her debut for England in 2021, scoring five times in her first six matches, including a hat-trick against Latvia. The tricky winger, who has a real eye for goal, has slotted in to Sarina Wiegman's plans with ease, putting in some fine early performances. Making the squad for Women's EURO 2022 would be a dream come true for Ella — one that she is on target to achieve.

STATS

BORN: 2 September, 1999 (Tyldesley)

POSITION: Midfielder/ Forward

CAPS: 11

GOALS: 6

DEBUT APPEARANCE: February 2021 v Northern Ireland

DEBUT GOAL: February 2021 v Northern Ireland

GETTING TO KNOW ELLA

During a two-year spell at Manchester City, Ella's role model was Lucy Bronze. She learnt from the way Lucy trained on the pitch and in the gym to become a top professional herself.

KEIRA WALSH

Lioness Lowdown:

Keira Walsh is a defensive midfielder whose vision and perfect passing make her one of the best technical players in the England Women squad. Her ability to read games and deliver accurate balls to her team-mates are often key to unlocking a game. Women's EURO 2022 is likely to be her second major tournament, after she featured at the 2019 Women's World Cup.

GETTING TO KNOW **KEIRA**
Keira and Leah Williamson have been best mates since they first met at an England U-15s camp.

STATS

BORN: 8 April, 1997 (Rochdale)

POSITION: Midfielder

CAPS: 37

GOALS: 0

DEBUT APPEARANCE: November 2017 v Kazakhstan

LEAH WILLIAMSON

Lioness Lowdown:

An important player in England's squad, Leah Williamson is equally good playing as a defender or in a defensive midfield role. Leah's England journey began with the U-15s side, before rising through the ranks to make her senior debut aged 21. Leah's proudest moment in a white shirt was when she captained England Women for the first time in September 2021, aged just 24.

GETTING TO KNOW **LEAH**

Leah once dreamed of becoming a track and field Olympian. Instead, her dream came true with Team GB's footballers.

STATS

BORN: 29 March, 1997 (Milton Keynes)

POSITION: Defender/Midfielder

CAPS: 27

GOALS: 2

DEBUT APPEARANCE: June 2018 v Russia

DEBUT GOAL: November 2019 v Czech Republic

LOTTE WUBBEN-MOY

Lioness Lowdown:

Lotte Wubben-Moy is a centre-back who is comfortable with the ball at her feet. A regular for the Young Lionesses, often wearing the captain's armband, Lotte could have chosen to play for the Netherlands through her Dutch father. Lotte's strengths are her ability to read the game, her physical fitness and her composure under pressure. When called for, she can also play as a defensive midfielder.

GETTING TO KNOW **LOTTE**
London-born Lotte believes her time at university in the USA built in her a winning mentality.

STATS

BORN: 11 January, 1999 (Nottingham)

POSITION: Defender

CAPS: 7

GOALS: 0

DEBUT APPEARANCE: February 2021 v Northern Ireland

KAREN BARDSLEY

STATS

BORN: 14 October, 1984 (Santa Monica, USA)

POSITION: Goalkeeper

CAPS: 81

DEBUT APPEARANCE: March 2005 v Northern Ireland

Lioness Lowdown:

England's No1 at three Women's World Cups and two European Women's Championships, goalkeeper Karen Bardsley is one of England's most experienced players, with more than 80 caps. Her first came 17 years ago!

MARY EARPS

STATS

BORN: 7 March, 1993 (London)

POSITION: Goalkeeper

CAPS: 15

DEBUT APPEARANCE: April 2014 v Montenegro

Lioness Lowdown:

A commanding goalkeeper with plenty of experience, Mary Earps is in the best form of her career. She has already earned double figures for caps and wore the No1 jersey in Sarina Wiegman's first squad.

ELLEN WHITE

STATS

BORN: 9 May, 1989 (Aylesbury)

POSITION: Forward

CAPS: 104

GOALS: 49

DEBUT APPEARANCE: March 2010 v Austria

DEBUT GOAL: March 2010 v Austria

Ellens' Story

Ellen grew up in a football-mad family and has played football since she was four. There weren't any girls' clubs, so Ellen's dad set up his own. Her story echoes that of many other women of her generation: Ellen was the team's only girl, yet she was never afraid to play against the bigger and stronger boys. Her next youth team was Aylesbury Town, before the youngster was scouted by Arsenal's academy, aged eight.

Ellen left Arsenal for London rivals Chelsea while studying for her A-levels, and was the Blues' top scorer three seasons in a row, all while still a teenager. At this time, becoming a professional footballer remained a dream, with Ellen focusing on her studies. The striker joined Leeds Carnegie, but was forced to take a spell on the sidelines following a serious knee injury. On her return, she scored twice in the final to help Leeds win the FA Women's Premier League Cup in 2010, the first of many trophies she would go on to win. The following month, Ellen earned her first call-up to England's senior squad, scoring her maiden international goal on debut.

Next, came a successful few seasons on her return to Arsenal, where Ellen won seven trophies, including three league titles. Ellen's first World Cup was at Germany 2011, after scoring four times in qualification. Her superb lob in the Group Stage against would-be world champions Japan was one of Ellen's most memorable goals. England progressed to the quarter-finals, only to lose to France in a penalty shoot-out.

Four years later, Ellen helped the Lionesses to a third place – and best ever – finish at the 2015 Women's World Cup in Canada, while it was at the 2019 Women's World Cup in France that White shone most brightly. Her six strikes saw her tie with USA stars Alex Morgan and Megan Rapinoe for the most goals scored, while Rapinoe was awarded the Golden Boot, having also claimed three assists. Her famous 'goggles' goal celebration went global, as

Ellen celebrates scoring against world champions the USA at the 2019 World Cup.

England Women inspired thousands of new fans, young and old, around the world.

The fantastic finisher has now starred for England for more than a decade, becoming the latest Lioness to win a century of caps. She describes being part of the squad as "an unbelievable feeling", and brings the same passion and excitement to each game as she did on her debut. At the time of writing, with 48 strikes to her name, Ellen is England's all-time record goalscorer, a number she expects to add to before hanging up her boots. With Women's EURO 2022 on home soil, expect more big goals from England's No9.

The striker has one of the most recognizable goal celebrations in the women's game.

BIG MATCH MOMENTS

Over the past few seasons, England Women and their fans have seen so many amazing matches and dramatic goals, moments that will live long in their memory. Here's a look back at just a few of them. Which one is your favourite?

2019

2019 was a massive year in England's history as millions of viewers cheered on the Lionesses. Strong team and individual performances saw the side win a trophy and reach the Women's World Cup semi-finals.

The Lionesses celebrate following their capture of the 2019 SheBelieves Cup.

Keeper Karen Bardsley makes a strong save to keep out Japan in the World Cup Group D match.

England's subs line up to celebrate Lucy Bronze's epic strike against Norway in the World Cup quarter-final match.

A 19-year-old Lauren Hemp wins her first senior cap against Portugal in October.

CHAMPIONS

Hotshot Ellen White scores the first of her six goals at the World Cup in France.

Coach Phil Neville consoles the squad after coming so close to making the World Cup final.

The record attendance for an England Women match is announced at the friendly against Germany in November.

77,768

51

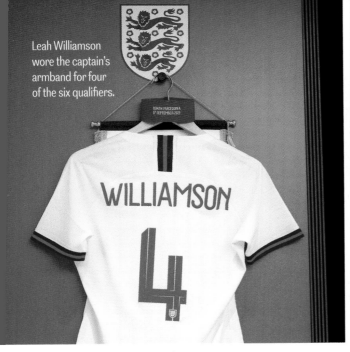

Leah Williamson wore the captain's armband for four of the six qualifiers.

Four new faces made their senior debut in February – Sandy MacIver, Ella Toone, Lotte Wubben-Moy and Ebony Salmon.

2021

With no matches in 2020 due to the COVID-19 global pandemic, England Women returned with a bang in 2021! Under new coach Sarina Wiegman, the Lionesses took maximum points from their six games in Women's World Cup qualifying with goals, goals and more goals on show!

Beth Mead gets to take the match ball home after becoming the first England Women player to score a hat-trick at Wembley.

Bethany England was a super scoring sub!

Ellen White celebrates her team's ninth goal against Latvia and becomes England's all-time leading goalscorer.

Ella Toone celebrates her own first senior international hat-trick, against Latvia in October.

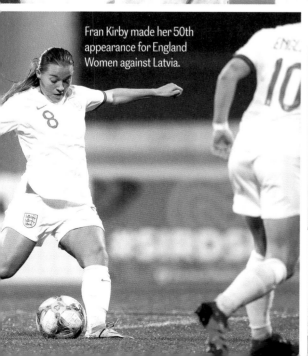

Fran Kirby made her 50th appearance for England Women against Latvia.

Sarina Wiegman made a flying start as England Women's new head coach.

LEGENDARY LIONESSES

Over the first 50 years in the history of England Women's senior side, many women will be remembered for their performances on the pitch and important work off it. Here are just a few pioneering players who have helped to pave the way for the next generations of women and girls, at home and around the world.

SYLVIA GORE

STATS
BORN: 25 November, 1944 (Prescot)
POSITION: Midfielder

Lioness Lowdown:

Sylvia Gore is a true history maker! She is remembered for being England Women's first-ever goalscorer in the first official match that England played in 1972, a year after the FA's ban on women's football had been lifted. In Greenock, the home team Scotland were 2-0 up before England fought back. Sylvia scored first, after making a 40-yard run and slipping the ball past the keeper. Two more goals followed to hand England an historic victory.

Born in Prescot, 12-year-old Sylvia started playing for girls' team Manchester Corinthians in the late 1950s. The pitches were poor back then and the post-match showers came courtesy of a bucket of cold water or a splash in the nearest duck pond! As a teenager she travelled the world, playing football in South America and Italy in front of huge crowds at a time when women's football was still outlawed in England. The attacking midfielder went on to have a long and successful career in football. It wasn't only at international level that Sylvia found the net – her goal-scoring instincts were so sharp that she once scored 134 times in a single season!

After retiring aged 36, Sylvia became a coach and a manager, working hard off the pitch to help make the women's game better. In 2000 she was awarded an MBE for services to girls' and women's football.

The first England women's national team lining up in 1972.

HOPE POWELL

Lioness Lowdown:

Hope Powell first made the news when FA rules banned her from representing her school's mixed team beyond the age of 11. She has been making headlines as a trailblazer of the women's game ever since. As a player, Hope won 66 caps for England Women between 1983 and 1998, scoring 35 times as a goal-hungry midfielder.

She began her coaching qualifications aged 19, becoming the first woman to earn the UEFA Pro Licence, the highest coaching award available. In June 1998, Hope was made the first-ever full-time England coach. She was also the first woman, first black woman and the nation's youngest-ever coach. Hope led England Women at two FIFA Women's World Cups and four UEFA Women's EUROs, over 15 years. Reaching the final of Women's EURO 2009 in Finland was a high point in the Lionesses' history.

Hope has helped to advance the women's game, battling to improve pay and facilities for her players, while raising the profile of women's sport. She was awarded an OBE and a CBE in recognition of her work, and was inducted into English football's Hall of Fame in 2003. Today, Hope continues to coach in the Women's Super League.

STATS

BORN: 8 December, 1966 (London)

POSITION: Midfielder

CAPS: 66

GOALS: 35

MARY PHILLIP

Lioness Lowdown:

Mary Phillip was born and raised in Peckham, South London. She played football from a young age and quickly learnt to ignore those who told her that it wasn't a game for girls – kicking a ball with her brothers and riding her bike were her favourite pastimes.

Mary joined Millwall Lionesses at the age of 12, where she won two trophies. At 18, Mary was called up to play for another team of Lionesses – England's 1995 Women's World Cup squad. The talented defender, who was four months pregnant at the time, was told the tournament would likely be her last. Mary has always had a habit of beating the odds, however.

The defender returned to England duty in 2002, after her second son was born. That same year, she was handed the captain's armband, becoming the first black woman to lead England. By this time, she was captain of Fulham, and one of the first women to turn professional in the UK. Mary led Fulham to a string of trophies, before earning more medals as part of Arsenal's backline.

China 2007 saw Mary become the first English woman to play at two World Cups. She retired the following year with 65 caps.

Mary has since taken her talents into coaching, and manages Peckham Town. The first female manager of a men's team in English football to win a cup, more chapters in her trailblazing story are yet to be written.

STATS

BORN: 14 March, 1977 (London)
POSITION: Defender
CAPS: 65

KELLY SMITH

Lioness Lowdown:

Kelly Smith is among the finest strikers the women's game has ever produced. In a playing career that spanned more than 20 years, Kelly made 117 appearances for her country, starring at three UEFA Women's EUROs and two FIFA Women's World Cups.

It all began at Garston Boys Club. Kelly, aged 7, was the team's top scorer and loved playing for her local side. Then one day, parents of opposition teams complained about a girl being allowed to play and Kelly was kicked out of the side. Rather than give up the game, Kelly and her father founded their own team instead, Pinner Girls. At 16, Kelly was scouted by Arsenal, and helped them win the league in her first season. A glittering career in the USA and three successful spells with Arsenal followed, as the striker smashed every goal-scoring record going.

Kelly's first cap for England came just days after her 17th birthday (her debut had to wait until after her GCSE exams), and she scored her first goal on her second appearance. From then on, Kelly became one of the Lionesses' most important players, setting the standards for the team. Her outstanding play and eye for goal saw her become England's second highest all-time goalscorer (after Ellen White) with 46 goals, as well as a role model for many young footballers.

STATS

BORN: 29 October, 1978 (Watford)

POSITION: Striker

CAPS: 117

GOALS: 46

RACHEL YANKEY

Lioness Lowdown:

Eight-year-old Rachel Yankey was so desperate to play the sport that she loved, she asked a barber to shave off her hair. Rachel then took her initials and reinvented herself as 'Ray'. Appearing as a boy gave her the freedom to express herself on the pitch, without any distractions. It was two years before anyone (other than her friends and the manager of her all-boys' team) discovered that Rachel was a girl, and she was made to leave the pitch before a cup final. She then found a girls' team, aged 10. A move to Arsenal at the age of 16 marked the beginning of the wizarding winger's senior career.

A year later in 1997, Rachel earned her first England cap, scoring on her debut against Scotland. After a loan spell from Arsenal to a Canadian club, the winger returned to join Fulham, and was registered as the first professional female footballer in England. There, she won five trophies before Fulham's women's team sadly folded.

Having missed out on Hope Powell's Women's EURO 2009 squad, Rachel returned in 2010 to become only the second player to win 100 England caps. By 2012, she had become the Lionesses' most capped player of all time, after making her 120th appearance.

STATS

BORN: 1 November, 1979 (London)

POSITION: Midfielder/ Forward

CAPS: 129

GOALS: 19

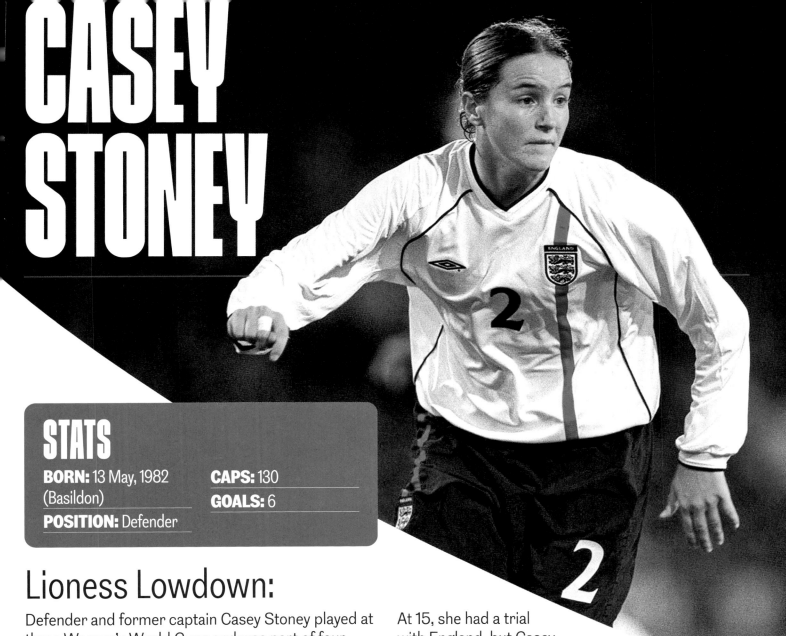

CASEY STONEY

STATS

BORN: 13 May, 1982 (Basildon)

POSITION: Defender

CAPS: 130

GOALS: 6

Lioness Lowdown:

Defender and former captain Casey Stoney played at three Women's World Cups and was part of four Women's EURO squads. Her 130 appearances put her among England's most-capped players ever.

Casey grew up in Essex, moving to south London towards the end of her primary school years. There, she joined a local boys' team, where she was the only girl in the whole league. Then, when she turned 11, rules at the time banned her from continuing to play mixed sports. Casey switched to play in a girls' league, but ran rings around the other players. When a scout from Chelsea invited Casey to train with them, the young footballer couldn't believe her luck. There was no junior team at Chelsea though, so Casey's teammates were all much older than her.

At 15, she had a trial with England, but Casey felt out of her depth. A rejection letter followed, but Casey was invited back soon after, and this time was selected for England Women's U-16s, then U-18s.

Her first senior cap came in 2000, with Casey determined to hold on to her England shirt. She started in central defence, before becoming the Lionesses' first-choice left-back. A natural leader, Casey was made captain by Hope Powell in 2012, and played for the Lionesses until 2017, describing her playing career as "more than a dream". Now Casey is successful from the sidelines, as a top women's coach.

ALEX SCOTT

STATS

BORN: 14 October, 1984 (London)

CAPS: 140

GOALS: 12

POSITION: Defender

Lioness Lowdown:

Proud East Londoner Alex Scott grew up playing in the 'cage' on her estate. Her skills saw her sign for Arsenal aged just eight, in the first of three trophy-laden spells with the Gunners. The right-back's first England cap came in 2004, while places in four Women's EUROs and three Women's World Cup squads followed. She retired as the Lionesses' second most-capped player of all time, and has gone on to forge a career as a TV football pundit and presenter.

STATS

BORN: 21 February, 1987 (Lagos, Nigeria)

POSITION: Forward

CAPS: 102

GOALS: 33

ENIOLA ALUKO

Lioness Lowdown:

Nigerian-born Eniola Aluko moved to Birmingham as a baby. She first joined the England youth ranks aged 14, and made her senior Lionesses debut at 17. Eni even sat an A-Level exam on the same day as playing a match at EURO 2005! The fearless goalscorer played for England at six major tournaments between 2005 and 2015, earning more than a century of caps. Since retiring, Eni has worked as a football club director in the UK and the US and as a TV pundit.

FARA WILLIAMS

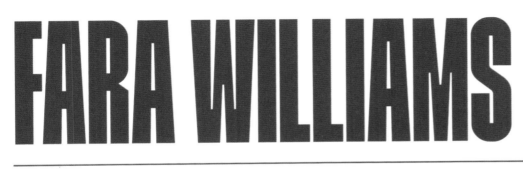

Lioness Lowdown:

Fara Williams' journey from growing up in Battersea, South London, to becoming England's most capped player – male or female – bears testimony to her inner strength. At 17, Fara found herself homeless, and would spend the next seven years in and out of hostels. The teenager hid her homelessness from her teammates, and even played at Women's EURO 2005 without sharing her secret. Her life changed when Everton boss Mo Marley gave her a contract to play for the club and a job as a coach.

Fara describes making her England debut, aged 17, as the proudest moment of her career. Over the following years, Fara became the heartbeat of the Lionesses' midfield, scoring important goals in major tournaments. England claimed third place at the 2015 FIFA Women's World Cup, beating Germany 1-0 in extra time, with Fara scoring the late penalty against their arch rivals.

STATS

BORN: 25 January, 1984 (London)
POSITION: Midfielder
CAPS: 172
GOALS: 40

After battling back from injury, Fara scored seven goals in qualification to make the 2011 Women's World Cup squad, scoring once at the finals. Her three goals at the next World Cup in Canada saw Fara finish as England's top scorer. This time, another Fara penalty was enough for England to beat Germany in the semis, securing bronze medals. In 2021, Fara retired from the game a legend, having played an astonishing 172 times for her country.

IN TRAINING

England training is where the hard work begins, as the Lionesses prepare for their big matches. But alongside the tactics and fitness drills, camp is where team spirit is built and friendships are formed.

Millie Bright marks skipper Steph Houghton a little too tightly!

Ellie Roebuck makes sure she's always on the winning team.

Rachel Daly displays some cool kick-up skills.

Hands up if you love scoring? It's a yes from Nikita Parris.

Sarina Wiegman gets to know young Lioness, Ebony Salmon.

Manchester club rivals, Ella Toone and Alex Greenwood are the best of friends at camp.

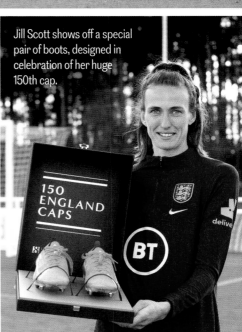

Jill Scott shows off a special pair of boots, designed in celebration of her huge 150th cap.

150 ENGLAND CAPS

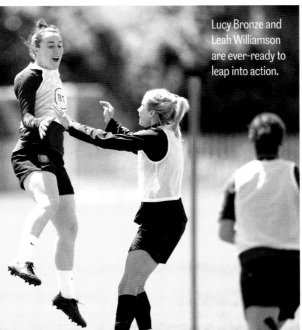

Lucy Bronze and Leah Williamson are ever-ready to leap into action.

Ellen White tries out a Golden Boot-winning celebration ahead of Women's EURO 2022.

63

YOUNG LIONESSES

Meet the next generation of players pushing for a regular place in England's senior squad. Some already have that special first cap, while others are set to grow into future starlets of the game. Join them on their journeys to the top!

NIAMH CHARLES

GETTING TO KNOW NIAMH
Former England and Liverpool legend Fara Williams was Niamh's hero growing up.

STATS

BORN: 21 June, 1999 (Wirral)
POSITION: Midfielder
DEBUT APPEARANCE: April 2021 v France

Lioness Lowdown:

Niamh Charles took up football aged 4, and joined a local grassroots team before being picked up by Liverpool's academy. A fantastic wide player, Niamh started out as a Lioness at U-17 level and so far has two caps for the senior side. She moved to current club Chelsea following Liverpool's relegation to the Championship in 2020.

HANNAH HAMPTON

Lioness Lowdown:

Hannah first tried on goalkeeper gloves for size as a nine year old. In 2013, she represented England's U-15s aged just 12, and advanced through every age group. Her first call-up for the senior squad came in March 2020 and Hannah now trains with the first team. While her full debut awaits, the talented stopper has her sights set on becoming England's No1 in the future.

GETTING TO KNOW **HANNAH**

Between the ages of five and 10, Hannah lived with her family in Spain, and played for Villareal's academy – as a forward!

STATS

BORN: 16 November, 2000 (Birmingham)

POSITION: Goalkeeper

LAUREN JAMES

STATS

BORN: 29 September, 2001 (London)

POSITION: Forward

Lioness Lowdown:

Lauren James first made a name for herself as a teenage scoring sensation with Manchester United. She loves to beat defenders and shoot from long range. Lauren has represented England at U-17 and U-19 level, and earned her first senior call up as part of a training camp in November 2020. Now with Chelsea, Lauren hopes her full England debut is not too far away.

GETTING TO KNOW **LAUREN**

Lauren is the younger sister of Chelsea and Three Lion's defender Reece James.

SANDY MACIVER

Lioness Lowdown:

Promising goalkeeper Sandy MacIver has already earned her first England cap, despite strong competition ahead of her. She helped the young Lionesses to win bronze at the U-20 Women's World Cup in 2018, claiming the Golden Glove as the tournament's best keeper. At club level, Sandy is Everton's No1. Look out for her flying saves!

GETTING TO KNOW **SANDY**

Sandy won a scholarship to an American university, where she played for the Clemson Tigers for three seasons.

STATS

BORN: 18 June, 1998 (Winsford)

POSITION: Goalkeeper

DEBUT APPEARANCE: February 2021 v Northern Ireland

ALESSIA RUSSO

STATS

BORN: 8 February, 1999 (Maidstone)

POSITION: Forward

DEBUT APPEARANCE: March 2020 v Spain

Lioness Lowdown:

A powerful striker who has been capped at every age group for England, Alessia Russo's first senior cap came in the 2020 SheBelieves Cup. Her progress since then has been hampered by injury, but now a professional player with Manchester United, Alessia is aiming to show her true potential in a Lionesses shirt.

GETTING TO KNOW **ALESSIA**

Alessia spent three seasons with US college side North Carolina Tar Heels before turning pro.

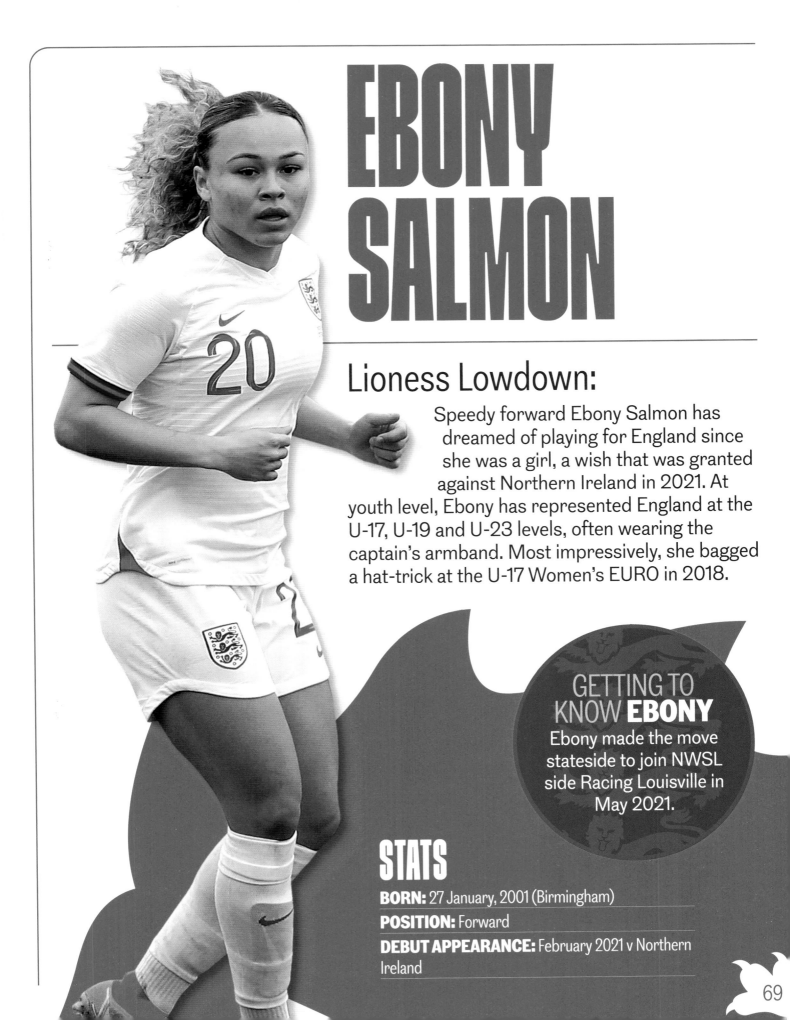

EBONY SALMON

Lioness Lowdown:

Speedy forward Ebony Salmon has dreamed of playing for England since she was a girl, a wish that was granted against Northern Ireland in 2021. At youth level, Ebony has represented England at the U-17, U-19 and U-23 levels, often wearing the captain's armband. Most impressively, she bagged a hat-trick at the U-17 Women's EURO in 2018.

GETTING TO KNOW EBONY

Ebony made the move stateside to join NWSL side Racing Louisville in May 2021.

STATS

BORN: 27 January, 2001 (Birmingham)

POSITION: Forward

DEBUT APPEARANCE: February 2021 v Northern Ireland

69

JESSICA CARTER

Lioness Lowdown:

Full-back Jess Carter can play in many positions, and has represented England's U-19, U-20 and U-21 Lionesses. Jess won her first senior England cap against Kazakhstan back in 2017, and has since been named in Sarina Wiegman's first senior squads. She has also played in a Champions League final for her club, Chelsea.

STATS

BORN: 27 October, 1997 (Warwick)
POSITION: Defender

STATS

BORN: 18 April, 2002 (Guernsey)
POSITION: Defender

MAYA LE TISSIER

Lioness Lowdown:

Guernsey-born Maya Le Tissier is a defender who has captained the England U-17 side at the UEFA Women's U-17 Championship, and now plays for the U-19 and U-23 Lionesses. An ambitious and athletic player, Maya is a natural leader on the pitch and is aiming to be better than Lucy Bronze one day.

ESME MORGAN

Lioness Lowdown:

Esme Morgan was called up for international duty back in April 2021, though her hopes of a senior England debut had to be put on hold after the defender broke her leg. At club level, Esme joined Manchester City's academy aged 14, and made her first team appearance after completing her GCSEs.

STATS

BORN: 18 October, 2000 (Sheffield)
POSITION: Defender

JESSICA PARK

Lioness Lowdown:

A natural goalscorer, Jess Park has represented England's U-17, U-19 and U-23 sides, scoring a combined 20 goals in her first 26 appearances. She joined Manchester City in 2017, where she can count many senior England Women among her team-mates. Jess is a bright young talent.

STATS

BORN: 21 October, 2001 (Brough)
POSITION: Forward

RECORD BREAKERS

Read on to discover some of the most important stats, records and milestones in the history of England Women's football. This is the Lionesses' story in numbers.

77,768
FANS WATCHED ENGLAND V GERMANY IN 2019 – A RECORD ATTENDANCE FOR A LIONESSES MATCH.

1881
THE YEAR ENGLAND PLAYED THEIR FIRST UNOFFICIAL INTERNATIONAL MATCH VERSUS SCOTLAND.

172
THE RECORD NUMBER OF ENGLAND CAPS EARNED BY MIDFIELD MAESTRO FARA WILLIAMS.

48
STAR STRIKER ELLEN WHITE LEADS THE PACK WHEN IT COMES TO ENGLAND GOALS.

20-0
ENGLAND'S BIGGEST WIN CAME AGAINST LATVIA ON 30 NOVEMBER, 2021.

10 ENGLAND'S LONGEST-SERVING SKIPPER FAYE WHITE CAPTAINED THE SIDE FOR A DECADE, FROM 2002-2012.

1972 THE YEAR ENGLAND'S FIRST OFFICIAL WOMEN'S INTERNATIONAL MATCH WAS CONTESTED. ENGLAND BEAT SCOTLAND 3-2.

50 THE NUMBER OF YEARS THAT WOMEN'S FOOTBALL WAS BANNED IN THE UK, FROM 1921-1971.

15 THE NUMBER OF YEARS HOPE POWELL SERVED AS MANAGER. (162 MATCHES)

9 UEFA WOMEN'S EURO APPEARANCES. ENGLAND'S NINTH, WOMEN'S EURO 2022, WILL BE AS HOSTS!

5 ENGLAND WOMEN APPEARANCES AT THE FIFA WOMEN'S WORLD CUP.

THE ULTIMATE LIONESSES QUIZ

Test your knowledge of the England Women's football team, the roaring Lionesses, in this quiz to find the ultimate fan. Aim for a score that will fill you with pride!

1. What colour is the team's away kit?

2. How many goals did striker Ellen White score at the 2019 FIFA Women's World Cup?

3. In which year did England play their first official international fixture?
a) 1872   b) 1921   c) 1972

Answers on page 78

4. Which young Lioness is pictured here?

5. Which England legend has made the most appearances for the senior side?

6. Which tournament, held in the United States, did England win in 2019?

7. Which team did England Women play at Wembley in 2019 in front of a record crowd?

8. Which of the following stadiums is not a Women's EURO 2022 venue?
a) Wembley Stadium   b) Villa Park
c) Old Trafford

9. Who was the first female coach of the England Women's senior squad?

10. Which forward became the first England Women's player to score a hat-trick at Wembley, in October 2021?

11. For how many years did Faye White serve as England captain?
a) Eight   b) Nine   c) Ten

12. What nationality is the England Women's head coach Sarina Wiegman?

HOW DID YOU SCORE?

1-4 correct answers
Some extra training is needed before you can join the squad of top England Women fans.

5-8 correct answers
Well played! You know your Millie Brights from your Ellen Whites!

9-12 correct answers
Be proud of your performance, you are an elite-level England fan!

GET INVOLVED!

If you've been inspired by the players in this book and don't already belong to a club or team, it's never too late to get started. You can join in by playing for a local grassroots club, whatever your ability, age or gender.

To find a team near you, plus information on more ways to enjoy the beautiful game, including coaching and refereeing, visit **www.the-fa.com/get-involved**.

Or if you'd rather stick to the sidelines, you can still play your part by cheering on the Lionesses – your positive support is key to helping England Women be the best that they can be. So pull on your shirt and wave those flags, whether you're supporting in the stadium or from home.
Come on, England!

ANSWERS

1. Red.
2. Six goals.
3. C – 1972.
4. Lauren Hemp.
5. Fara Williams.
6. The SheBelieves Cup.
7. Germany.
8. B – Villa Park.
9. Hope Powell.
10. Beth Mead.
11. Ten.
12. The Netherlands.